The Pleasure of Your Company

AN HORS D'OEUVRE COLLECTION

BY
NONNIE HOWELL
AND
DIANE PHILLIPS

- **OVER 100 TASTY RECIPES**
- **PARTY PLANNING GUIDE COMPLETE WITH MENUS**

Dedication

This book is dedicated to our good friends who have helped make this book a realization. A special thanks to Bill Cates, our publisher, for convincing us we could do it!

Acknowledgements

- Cover design by Jim Haynes.

- "Pixie" happy faces used with permission from Pinnacle Merchandise Co., Carlsbad, Calif. 92008

- Interior art work by Debra McNabb.

- Typesetting by Apostrophe, Inc., Rockville, MD.

LIBRARY OF CONGRESS NUMBER: 81-83400

ISBN 0-942 320-01-8

Published by: WRC Publishing
2915 Fenimore Road
Silver Spring, Maryland
20902

"Cookbooks Tastefully Published"

Foreword

We have entitled this book "The Pleasure of Your Company" because that's what it's all about; giving parties and seeing friends enjoy themselves. Our friends have encouraged us to write a cookbook so they can have all our recipes in one place! We are starting out with our favorite food - the hors d'oeuvre (it literally means "out of work" in French).

We became friends in 1974 when our husbands were stationed aboard the USS-JASON in San Diego, California. During that time, and since then, we have enjoyed sharing, and experimenting with different recipes. We both feel that it is indeed a compliment when a guest asks for a recipe. We give thanks to our friends who have shared their recipes with us.

If you spend hours agonizing over what to have for your parties or get-togethers, we have outlined a party guide along with different menus that may help you.

When you cook don't be afraid to use your instincts and imagination — add or subtract ingredients and see what happens! We have suggested ideas for giving parties. However, the biggest hint is to allow ample time for preparation — be organized, and cook as much as possible ahead of time.

So many cookbooks are used for just a few recipes. In this book we have compiled an excellent selection of hors d'oeuvre. We have used all the recipes at our parties. You can also use the recipes in this book for a quiet Saturday night sit-by-the-fire casual dinner with your family (sample menus are outlined). Freeze the leftovers for quick snacks.

We hope you use and enjoy these recipes as much as we have. They are for The Pleasure of Your Company!

Nonnie Howell — McLean, Virginia

Diane Phillips — San Diego, California

The Pleasure of Your Company
makes a great gift

To order additional copies
send $5.95, plus $1.00 for postage and handling to

The Pleasure of Your Company
P.O. Box 4011
Washington, D.C. 20815

Make check or money order payable to
WRC Publishing

Contents

DIPS FOR TORTILLA CHIPS.........................9
Tortilla Chips...................................10
Artichoke Cheese Dip.............................10
Guacamole I.....................................11
Guacamole II....................................11
Chili Cheese Dip................................11
Chili Con Queso.................................12
Hot Bean Dip....................................12
Broccoli-Mushroom-Cheese Dip....................13
A Colorful Mexican Dip..........................14
Frito Beef-Bean Chili Dip.......................14
Tostada Dip.....................................15

VEGETABLE DIPS AND SPREADS...................17
Swiss Cheese Dip................................18
Tuna — Onion Spread.............................18
Mustard Dip.....................................19
Curry Dip.......................................19
Cucumber Dip....................................20
Dill Weed Dip...................................20

DIPS AND SPREADS............................21
Sausage Treats..................................22
Rumaki Spread...................................22
Spinach Dip.....................................23
Braunschweiger Spread Dip.......................23
Mango Chutney Cheese Pate.......................24
Chipped Beef Spreads............................25

CHEESES.....................................27
Fresh Garlic Herb Cheese........................28
Beef Cheese Ball................................28
Holiday Cheese Ball.............................29
Cheese 'N Chutney Ball..........................29

FINGER FOODS................................31
Phyllo Dough....................................32
Curried Mushroom Rolls..........................33
Cheese Rolls....................................34

Crab Rolls..34
Spinach Rolls.......................................35
Armenian Canapes...................................35
Potato Skins.......................................36
Crabmeat Canapes...................................36
Spinach Squares....................................37
Polynesian Chicken Wings...........................37
Nachos...38
Lumpia With Shrimp and Pork........................39
Zucchini Bars......................................40
Artichoke Squares..................................40
Broiled Chicken On Rye.............................41
Sausalito Sour Doughs..............................41
Smoked Salmon And Boursin On Cucumbers.............42
Zucchini Rounds....................................42
Cheese Toast Canapes...............................43
Mexican Pinwheels..................................43
Chili Cheese Squares...............................44
Quiche Lorraine....................................45
Zucchini Quiche....................................46
Avocado-Crab Quiche................................47
Curried Tuna.......................................48
Shrimp Filling For Cherry Tomatoes.................48
Asparagus Rolls....................................49
Bacon-Cheese Toast Canapes.........................49

SPEAR IT WITH A TOOTHPICK.....................51
Artichokes In Blue Cheese 52
Bacon Wraps..52
Olive Wraps..52
Mexican Meatballs..................................53
Spinach Chicken With Oriental Dip..................54
Hawaiian Sausage Balls.............................55
Celery Victor......................................56
Supreme Sausages 56
Korean Beef With Vegetables........................57
Stuffed Mushrooms..................................57
Bacon-Cheese Mushrooms.............................58
Cheese-Nut Mushrooms...............................58
Oriental Mushrooms.................................59
Blue-Pecan Mushrooms...............................59
Bacon-Mushroom Wraps...............................60
Marinated Mushrooms................................60

HORS D'OEUVRE de MER 61
Mornay Sauce For Crab Claws And Large Shrimp 62
Sour Dough Shrimp Dip 63
Crab And Water Chestnut Spread 63
Crabmeat Cocktail Block 64
Crab-Artichoke-Mushroom Appetizer 65
Shrimp Or Crab Mold 66
Avocado Crab Dip 66
Pink Shrimp Mousse 67
Salmon Party Log 67
Hot Cheese-Crab 68
Clam Dip For Potato Chips 68
Crab-Clam Spread 69
King Crab Spread 69
Fruits De Mer 70
Oysters Bluepoint 70
Parmesan-Garlic Shrimp 71
Seviche 72

SPUR OF THE MOMENT HORS D'OEUVRES 73
Salami — Onion Rolls 74
Ham Pinwheels 74
Sherried Dates 74
Party Mix 75
Easy Escargots 75
Bricks Of Cream Cheese 76
Susan's Zucchini Snacks 76

THE SWEET PART OF THE PARTY 77
Amaretto Fondue 78
Chocolate Fondue 78
Fruit Boat 78
Petite Pecan Tarts 79
Caramel Brownies 79
Cheesecake Squares 80
Almond Roca 81
Peanut Butter Chocolate Bars 81
Peppermint Brownies 82
Pineapple Fluff dip 83
Chocolate Cups 83
Brownie Mounds 84
Apricot Squares 85
Strawberry Fundue 86

MISCELLANEOUS 87
    Cream Cheese Pastry Crust. .88
    Sweet And Sour Sauce. 88
    Green Chili Salsa. 89

PARTY PLANNING. 91
    Guidelines For Party Planning. 92
    Party Planner Menus. 93-95
    Quiet "Sit-By-The-Fire Dinner" For 4-6. 96
    For the Teen Scene — Favorites For The Fussy. 97

Dips for Tortilla Chips

Tortilla Chips

First a word about the chips. Almost as popular as a cracker, tortilla corn chips are a must for a party and the following recipes are great companions for them. If you cannot go to a nearby tortilla factory and buy big fresh bags of corn chips the next best thing is to fry your own at home. Buy fresh corn tortillas at a supermarket in 10-ounce packages. Cut them into six to eight wedges. Fill a dutch oven pot (large pot) ⅓ full with oil. You can fry one half of a package of chips at one time. When oil is hot slowly slide chips in and fry until crisp (1-2 minutes). Remove from pot with a large slotted spoon. Drain on paper towels. Salt is optional. Store in airtight containers.

Dorito brand regular flavored corn chips are very good because they are not too salty.

Artichoke Cheese Dip

A quick, fun and deeeelicious dip.

1	8 ½-ounce can of artichoke hearts, drained
1	cup real mayonnaise
1	cup pure Parmesan cheese, grated
	dash or two of garlic powder

Cut artichoke hearts into bite size pieces. Mix with mayonnaise, cheese and garlic. Spread into a quiche dish or similar baking pan.

Bake, in conventional oven, only until heated through (about 10-15 minutes at 350°). Fast cooking or overbaking tends to separate the dip!

1st variation: Add 1 can crabmeat. Top with breadcrumbs before baking.

2nd variation: In place of 1 cup Parmesan, use,

½	cup grated Swiss and
½	cup grated Parmesan

Serve hot.

Guacamole I

2   large fully ripened, avocados
2   heaping tablespoons sour cream
½   teaspoon lemon juice
     garlic powder to taste
¼   cup green chili salsa (page 89)
     salt and pepper to taste

Blend ingredients with electric mixer. Serve with tortilla chips.

Guacamole II

2   ripened avocados
1   tomato diced
1   chopped green onion
1   teaspoon lemon juice
1   tablespoon La Victoria Salsa Ranchera
     garlic salt to taste

Blend well, and serve.

Chili Cheese Dip

2   cans of Hormel Chili with No Beans
12   ounces extra sharp Cheddar cheese, grated
1   8-ounce package cream cheese
¼   cup chopped white onions

In a double boiler heat the above until blended well. Serve in chafing dish.

Chili Con Queso

There are so many variations, but this is a must.

2	tablespoons butter
1	clove of garlic, mashed
¼	cup milk
½	pound American cheese, grated
¾	pound Swiss cheese, grated
1	medium onion, chopped fine
1	cup of canned tomatoes
2-4	ounces diced green chilis (canned)
	to taste: salt, celery salt, cayenne, paprika

Melt butter over low heat and add garlic, cooking til soft. Add milk and cheese. Cook until cheeses are melted. Add remaining ingredients and stir well to break up tomatoes and chilis. Heat through.
Serve in chafing dish.

Hot Bean Dip

1	10 ½-ounce can of Frito's Jalapeno Bean Dip
8	ounces of sour cream
8	ounces of cream cheese
½	package of taco seasoning
1/8	teaspoon tabasco
3	ounces Monterey Jack cheese, grated
3	ounces Cheddar cheese, grated

Mix the first 5 ingredients and spread into a baking dish. Top with grated Monterey Jack and grated Cheddar cheese.
Bake until heated through.

Broccoli-Mushroom-Cheese Dip

3	tablespoons vegetable oil
3	stalks celery, chopped
1	medium-large onion, chopped
½	pound fresh mushrooms, sliced
1	medium-large bunch fresh broccoli, chopped
1	can cream of mushroom soup
1	8-ounce jar Kraft Cheez-Whiz
1½	teaspoons lemon juice
1	clove fresh garlic, mashed
¼	teaspoon worcestershire
2	tablespoons sherry
	salt and pepper to taste

Sauté the celery and onions in 3 tablespoons of oil. Drain with slotted spoon and set aside. Sauté the mushrooms in same pan. Drain and set aside. In a large pot cook the broccoli in an inch of boiling water. Cook only until barely tender - be careful not to burn! Drain and return to pot. Stir in mushroom soup and Cheez-Whiz. Mix until cheese is melted. Add celery, onions and mushrooms. Stir in remaining ingredients. Season to taste. Serve heated.

Note: If you double the recipe do not double the soup. One can is sufficient. This dip freezes well!

A Colorful Mexican Dip

Almost like a thick gazpacho

¾-1   pound Monterey Jack cheese, grated
1   medium cucumber, deseeded and chopped
5   medium fully ripe tomatoes, chopped
4-7   ounces diced green chilis
4   green onions, chopped
2   tablespoons fresh parsley, chopped
1   small can chopped black olives
1   (8-ounce) bottle of Lowery's Italian
    With Cheese Salad Dressing
    Optional: Small chunks of fresh
    avocados (add just before serving)

Toss ingredients. Chill.

Frito Beef-Bean Chili Dip

1   pound ground beef, browned
1   medium onion, chopped
1-3   tablespoons green pepper chopped
1   tablespoon chopped parsley
½-1   teaspoon salt
½-1   teaspoon pepper
1   teaspoon chili powder
1   small can tomato paste
1   can pinto beans
1   can chili with no beans
1   cup or more grated Cheddar cheese
1   7-ounce jar green olives with pimentos

Brown ground beef then drain any grease. Add onion, green pepper, parsley, salt, pepper, chili powder and tomato paste. In food processor mix together pinto beans and chili, using steel blade. Pour into beef mixture. Mix well. Spread into a 9"x13" baking dish.

Bake at 350° 35-45 minutes. Top with Cheddar and sliced olives. Dip with tortilla chips.

Tostada Dip

Easy, fun and so good!

24 ounces refried beans (canned)
8 ounces sour cream
2 ripe avocados mashed well
2 cups shredded lettuce
3 medium tomatoes, chopped
8 ounces Cheddar cheese, grated
4 ounces green chili salsa (page 89)
  large corn tortilla chips for dipping

Spread refried beans into a two quart rectangular dish or large platter. Follow in order with layers of sour cream, avocados, lettuce, tomatoes, cheese and salsa. Scoop with corn chips!

Optional: add sliced black olives and chopped green pepper to layers.

15

Vegetable Dips and Spreads

Swiss Cheese Dip

This is an excellent "fondue" for raw vegetables!

1   cup, firmly packed, aged Swiss cheese, grated
¾   cup chopped white onions
1   cup real mayonnaise

Mix ingredients. Heat through. Do not overcook or mixture will separate.

Variation: By using a combination of cheeses, this becomes an excellent spread for crackers. Suggested cheeses: Gouda, Muenster, Cheddar (mild or sharp) and Monterey Jack.

Serving Suggestion: Serve hot in a hollowed out sourdough bread loaf. When dip is gone, slice the breadboat and place under broiler.

Tuna — Onion Spread

1   envelope Lipton Onion Soup Mix
2   cups sour cream
1   6-ounce can tuna, drained and flaked
½   cup chopped cucumber
1   small carrot grated
2   teaspoons chopped parsley

Mix all ingredients and chill. Spread on favorite crackers or dip with potato chips. Great vegetable dipper!

Mustard Dip

Use with pretzels too!

1	cup real mayonnaise
½	pint heavy cream, whipped
½	cup Dijon mustard

Combine ingredients. Refrigerate overnight.

Curry Dip

1	cup of real mayonnaise
½-1	teaspoon curry powder
½	teaspoon garlic salt
2	tablespoons chopped onion
1	tablespoon horseradish
1	tablespoon vinegar

Blend all ingredients. Refrigerate until seasoned.

Cucumber Dip

1   cup seeded and well drained cucumbers*
¼   cup mayonnaise
1   teaspoon vinegar
1   tablespoon grated onion
1   tablespoon chopped parsley
½   cup sour cream

Chop cucumber with steel blade in food processor. Mix with remaining ingredients. Add salt and pepper to taste. Dip with chips or vegetables.

*It is best to use a hybrid cucumber because they are seedless, bitterless and "burpless". You can use the skin and all! For this recipe you would use one-half of a large hybrid cucumber. They are available at most grocery stores.

Dill Weed Dip

1   tablespoon dill weed
1   tablespoon dried minced onion
1   tablespoon dried parsley
2   teaspoons Spice Islands Beau Monde
      seasoning
1   cup sour cream
1   cup real mayonnaise

Lightly mix all ingredients together. Refrigerate overnight to season ingredients. Dip with raw vegetables.

Holiday hint: The dried ingredients may be mixed and jarred for holiday gifts. Mix equal parts of dillweed, minced onion, dried parsley and Beau Monde seasoning. Then include a recipe card stating to mix 3 tablespoons of mixture to 1 cup of sour cream and 1 cup of mayonnaise.

Dips and Spreads

Sausage Treats

  1   pound sausage (Sweet Italian or hot pork
      sausage)
  1   pound ground beef
  1   pound Velveeta cheese, cut up
1-2   loaves Party Rye bread

Fry sausage and then drain. Chop in food processor. Fry beef and drain. Chop in food processor.

Return meats to skillet and add Velveeta. Add salt, pepper and garlic to taste. Cook until cheese melts. Toast rye rounds on one side. Spread the other side with the meat mixture.

Bake in 325° oven until heated through.

Rumaki Spread

For liver lovers

  1   stick butter
  ½   pound chicken livers
  1   tablespoon soy sauce
  ½   teaspoon onion salt
  ½   teaspoon dry mustard
  ¼   teaspoon nutmeg
  1   can water chestnuts, drained and finely
      chopped
  6   slices crisp bacon, crumbled
  2   fresh green onions, thinly sliced

Melt butter in a skillet and cook chicken livers until slightly pink inside. Transfer to a blender and add soy sauce, onion salt, mustard, and nutmeg. Blend until smooth. To creamed mixture fold in 1/2 of the water chestnuts and bacon.

Refrigerate mixture at least two hours. Let soften at room temperature an hour before serving. Top with layers of water chestnuts, bacon and green onions.

Serve with rice crackers.

Spinach Dip

1   package frozen chopped spinach thawed and drained well
4   ounces of Kraft Blue Cheese
1   tablespoon onion, grated fine
1   tablespoon mayonnaise

Press spinach well to remove liquid. Blend in cheese, onion and mayonnaise. Mix with spinach. Chill for at least two hours. Serve with Bremner unsalted crackers.

Braunschweiger Spread Dip

8   ounces Braunschweiger (liver sausage)
¼   cup sour cream
¼   cup mayonnaise
¼   cup chopped green peppers
1   tablespoon chopped onions
4   drops tabasco sauce

Combine ingredients and mix thoroughly. Goes great on Party Rye bread — or your favorite cracker.

Mango Chutney Cheese Paté

3	ounces cream cheese, softened
½	cup grated Cheddar cheese
2	teaspoons dry sherry
¼-½	teaspoon curry powder
	dash of salt
¼-½	cup finely chopped mango chutney
2	green onions finely chopped

Beat cream cheese until fluffy. Mix in Cheddar, sherry, curry and salt. Spread, ½ inch thick, on to a fancy plate. Spread with chutney. Top with green onions. Serve with Wheat Thins.

Note: Indian Mango Chutney is hot (spicy).

Chipped Beef Spreads

Hot Spread:

8 ounces cream cheese
8 ounces sour cream
1 3 ounce package of chipped beef or
  1 small jar of Armour dried beef, chopped
½ cup chopped green pepper
1 small onion, chopped
  Optional: ¼ teaspoon garlic powder
  ¼ teaspoon seasoned salt

Mix ingredients and spread into baking dish. Top with 4 ounces of chopped pecans mixed with 1 tablespoon of butter.
Bake at 350° for 20 minutes. Serve heated with Triscuits.

Optional: Dollop with green chili salsa.

Cold Spread:

¼ cup real mayonnaise
¼ cup sour cream
¼ cup chopped green onions
8 ounces cream cheese
2-3 ounces chopped chipped or dried beef
½ cup grated Parmesan cheese
  Optional: chopped nuts for garnish

Mix ingredients and spread into a small dish or roll into a ball. Serve chilled with favorite crackers.

Cheeses

Fresh Garlic Herb Cheese

8   ounces cream cheese
3   tablespoons lemon juice
½   teaspoon dried savory
¼   teaspoon fresh ground pepper
2   cloves garlic, crushed

Beat ingredients with electric mixer. Spread mixture in a small fancy glass bowl. Serve when well chilled. Spread on Bremmer crackers.

Beef Cheese Ball

8   ounces cream cheese, softened
1   small package chipped beef or 1 small jar dried
     beef
2   teaspoons prepared mustard
1   tablespoon horseradish
2   tablespoons milk

Chop beef in food processor and mix half of it with cream cheese, mustard, horseradish and milk. Roll mixture in remaining beef. Serve with Bremmer unsalted crackers. Also, excellent with pretzels.

Holiday Cheese Ball

1   small jar Kraft Roca Bleu Cheese
1   small jar Kraft Pimento Cheese
8   ounces cream cheese
    dash of tabasco
6   ounces chopped walnuts

Mix cheeses and tabasco with electric mixer. Roll in chopped walnuts. Chill before serving.

Cheese 'N Chutney Ball

4   ounces Kraft Blue Cheese
8   ounces cream cheese
¼   cup chopped chutney
6   ounces toasted almonds, chopped

Blend cheeses and chutney. Roll in almonds. Chill.

Finger Foods

A Word About Phyllo Dough

Phyllo dough, or filo dough, is a paper thin strudel-type pastry used for making wonderful hors d'oeuvre as well as main dishes and pastries (such as Baklava). Phyllo, pronounced fee-lo, can be purchased fresh or frozen at Greek grocery stores, or at most Gourmet specialty-type grocery stores. A pound of phyllo will make between 75 and 100 hors d'oeuvre, which can be frozen and baked directly from the freezer. Sheets of phyllo must be kept covered with a moist (not wet) towel (long paper towels will work), while you are working with them. Frozen phyllo dough keeps for several months in the freezer. Thaw overnight in the refrigerator. There are different ways to roll phyllo, the flag- type triangle being the most popular. Directions for the rolling are on the packages that you buy. The following recipes for the phyllo dough are time consuming, but the praise you will receive makes it worth the effort.

When using fillings that contain liquids (e.g. mushroom curry) it is recommended that you sprinkle the dough with superfine bread crumbs after buttering, prior to rolling. This helps avoid possible seepage.

Our recipes are mostly for the rolled version, but again the flag-type triangle is fun to do for variation.

Curried Mushroom Rolls

          1   pound chopped mushrooms
          ½   cup minced green onions
          ¾   cup butter
          3   tablespoons flour
          ½   teaspoon salt
          ¼   teaspoon curry powder
          ½   cup evaporated milk
          1   pound phyllo dough

Chop mushrooms and onions in food processor using steel blade.
Sauté mushrooms and onions in butter until mushrooms are softened. Reduce heat to low, stir in flour, salt and curry powder, and cook until thickened. Add evaporated milk. Cook until thickened. Cool. Have ready 1-pound of phyllo dough and 1 cup melted butter. Cut phyllo dough into three equal parts. On separate strips, place 1 teaspoon cooled filling at the end, fold over, brush long end with butter, fold in sides, roll up. Brush top and bottom with butter.
Bake at 350° for 10-15 minutes. Can be frozen uncooked.

Helpful hint: Sprinkle phyllo lightly with finely chopped bread crumbs after brushing it with the butter, prior to rolling. This helps avoid seepage.

Cheese Rolls

¼ cup grated Parmesan cheese
½ pound Feta cheese
½ pound cottage cheese
3 ounces softened cream cheese
3 eggs
1 pound phyllo dough
½-¾ cup melted butter

Mix all ingredients except phyllo and butter. Cut phyllo into 3 equal parts. Place 1 teaspoon filling at the short end of phyllo. Brush phyllo with butter. Fold in sides, brush with butter, roll up, and brush top and bottom with butter.
Bake at 350° 'til golden, about 20 minutes.

Note: If you wish to freeze, do so before baking.

Crab Rolls

1 6 to 8-ounce package crab meat
2 tablespoons butter
¼ cup chopped green onions
½ cup chopped mushrooms
1 cup shredded Monterey Jack cheese
1 3 ounce package cream cheese, softened
⅓ cup mayonnaise
2 tablespoons minced parsley
1 teaspoon horseradish
1 teaspoon worchestershire sauce
½ pound phyllo dough

Drain and chop crab. Melt butter in skillet, add mushrooms and onions, and saute for 2 minutes. Combine remaining ingredients in a large bowl. Add mushrooms, and stir well. Have ½ pound phyllo dough, and ½ cup melted butter ready.
Cut phyllo dough into 3 equal parts. Place one teaspoon filling at end of pastry. Fold up once, turn in sides, brush with butter, and roll up. Bake at 350° for 20 minutes, or til golden.

Note: If you wish to freeze, do so before baking.

Spinach Rolls

1   pound fresh spinach, cooked, and chopped or
    1 package frozen chopped spinach defrosted
    and squeezed dry
¼ cup olive oil
1   onion finely chopped
1   cup Feta cheese
3   eggs, lightly beaten
½ pound phyllo dough
½ pound melted butter

Saute onion in olive oil. Beat eggs, and add eggs, onions, salt and pepper to spinach and mix well. Add Feta and mix lightly. Cut phyllo into 3 equal parts. Place a small tablespoon of spinach mixture at one end, fold up once, turn in sides, and roll. Brush with butter.

Bake at 350°, 15 minutes or until browned. Cool slightly. Serve.

Note: These may be frozen before baking. Bake at 350° for 20-25 minutes if frozen.

Armenian Canapes

½ pound Monterey Jack cheese
½ bunch of fresh parsley, chopped fine
2   eggs beaten
    phyllo dough
    real butter

Lightly butter a 9"x13" pan. With pastry brush, lightly butter each layer of phyllo dough (6-8 layers). Put parsley, cheese, then the eggs on top of the last layer of phyllo.

Bake about 25 minutes at 350°. Let set before cutting into small squares.

Potato Skins

large baking potatoes, scrubbed well
fully cooked bacon strips
grated Cheddar cheese
Marie's Blue Cheese Salad Dressing
sour cream
*Optional — chopped green onions

Bake potatoes fully. Fry bacon and drain. Cut cooled potatoes into eight sections. Scoop out white potato meat leaving about ⅓ of an inch on each skin. Sprinkle with grated Cheddar cheese and crumbled bacon. Place under broiler until cheese melts. Serve hot with a small bowl of Marie's Blue Cheese Dressing mixed with sour cream to taste, for dipping.

Variation: Use Ranch Dressing for dipping or plain sour cream mixed with chives.

Crabmeat Canapes

12	ounces crabmeat
8	ounces cream cheese
¼	cup mayonnaise
2	egg yolks
1	small onion, finely chopped
¼	teaspoon prepared mustard
	dash of salt
8-10	slices of white bread, crusts removed

Mix crab and mayonnaise in a separate bowl. Set aside. In another bowl mix cream cheese, egg yolks, onion, mustard and salt. Beat with electric mixer. Butter one side of bread slices. Place under broiler 'til browned. Cut slices into four squares. On uncooked side place a dollop of crab. Top with creamed mixture. Broil 'til bubbly.

Spinach Squares

2   10-ounce packages of frozen chopped spinach
3   tablespoons butter
1   small onion, chopped fine
½   pound fresh mushrooms, chopped
4   eggs
¼   cup fine bread crumbs
1   can cream of mushroom soup
½   cup grated Parmesan cheese
1/8   teaspoon pepper
¼   teaspoon dry basil
¼   teaspoon oregano

Squeeze thawed spinach to remove water. Melt butter and sauté spinach, adding onions and mushrooms. In a bowl, beat the eggs with a whisk. Stir in bread crumbs, mushroom soup, 3 tablespoons of the cheese, spices and the spinach mixture. Blend well. Turn into a greased (8"x8") baking pan. Sprinkle with remaining cheese.

Bake uncovered at 325° for 35 minutes. Cool slightly. Cover and refrigerate. Cut into squares. Serve chilled or at room temperature.

Polynesian Chicken Wings

1-3   pounds of chicken wings

Marinade:

2   tablespoons of vegetable oil
1   cup of honey
½   cup of soy sauce
2   tablespoons of ketchup
   cornstarch to thicken

Cook the marinade over low heat until thickened, stirring often. Marinate chicken wings in sauce overnight or for several hours. Remove from marinade. Place chicken on baking sheets.

Bake at 350° 30-45 minutes, basting occasionally and turning over at least once.

Nachos

A simple microwave recipe

Spread corn tortilla chips on plate. Top with grated Cheddar/and or Monterey Jack cheese.

Heat in microwave until cheese melts. Remove from microwave and top with sour cream, guacamole, diced tomatoes and chopped ripe olives. Garnish around the chips with shredded lettuce.

Best if eaten right away.

Variation: Steak nachos — Add sauteed steak chunks to chips before placing in microwave.

Lumpia With Shrimp And Pork

Made easiest with help from a food processor!

1	tablespoon oil
¾	cup chopped fine celery
¾-1	pound boneless Pork roast, chopped fine
1	tablespoon Chinese rice wine
1	tablespoon soy sauce
½	teaspoon sugar
2	teaspoons salt
½	teaspoon M.S.G.
¾	pound fresh raw shrimp, chopped fine
10	medium mushrooms chopped fine
¼	pound fresh bean sprouts, chopped fine
1	tablespoon cornstarch
	Phillipine lumpia wrappers

In a wok or large skillet heat 1 tablespoon of oil and stir fry the celery for about a minute. Add the ground pork and cook until it loses its reddish color. Then add the wine, soy sauce, sugar, salt, MSG, shrimp and mushrooms. Stir fry until heated through and shrimp are cooked. Remove from heat.

Add chopped bean sprouts. Spoon out about 3 tablespoons of liquid and mix it with 1 tablespoon of cornstarch. Blend until smooth and then coat the meat mixture with a light glaze. Transfer to a large bowl and cool to room temperature.

Roll in Phillipine lumpia wrappers (small size). Freeze at this point if storing, or fry in hot oil until browned. Can be reheated in a 350° oven 10-15 minutes. Serve with soy sauce, Chinese Mustard, and Sweet-sour sauce.

Zucchini Bars

3 cups thinly sliced zucchini
1 medium onion, chopped
3 large garlic cloves, mashed
3 tablespoons finely chopped parsley
½ teaspoon oregano flakes
½ teaspoon salt
½ cup salad oil
½ cup Parmesan cheese, grated
4 eggs, slightly beaten
1 cup Bisquick
½ cup green chili salsa (page 89)

Mix the first ten ingredients together. Spread into a greased 13"x9" pan. Spoon spread green chili salsa over mixture.

Bake at 375° for 25-30 minutes or until slightly browned. Take out of oven and sprinkle with additional Parmesan. Serve warm or chilled.

Artichoke Squares

2   6-ounce jars marinated artichoke hearts
4   eggs
1½ cups bread crumbs
1   medium onion, chopped
8   ounces grated sharp Cheddar cheese
¼   cup green chili salsa (page 89)
    salt and pepper to taste
    garlic powder to taste

Drain the artichoke hearts, saving the liquid. Cut up hearts. Combine all ingredients, including the liquid from the artichoke hearts. Place in square baking dish.

Bake at 350° for 35-40 minutes.

Broiled Chicken On Rye

2   cups of chopped cooked chicken
¾   cup pitted black olives, sliced thin
½   cup real mayonnaise
4   ounces shredded Cheddar cheese
1   small onion, chopped
⅓   cup green pepper, chopped
     dash or two of tabasco
2   egg whites, stiffly beaten
1   loaf dark Party Rye bread

Mix chicken, olives, mayonnaise, cheese, onion, green pepper and tabasco. Fold in egg whites. Spread mixture on to Party Rye bread. Broil until cheese melts. Serve immediately.

Sausalito Sour Doughs

8   ounces crabmeat
¼   cup diced celery
½   cup Cheddar cheese or Monterey Jack cheese, grated
½   cup mayonnaise
4   sour dough muffins slightly toasted

Combine crab, celery, onions, cheese and mayonnaise. Spread on lightly buttered muffins. Broil until bubbly. Cut into quarters.

try this

Smoked Salmon And Boursin On Cucumbers

      2   hot house (hybrid) cucumbers, sliced
      1   pound herbed Boursin cheese (or use Fresh
          Garlic Herb Cheese recipe on page 28)
 ¼-½   pound smoked salmon
          fresh parsley

Spread cheese on cucumber rounds. Cut salmon in thin strips and criss cross on top of Boursin. Garnish with small parsley leaf. Serve chilled.

Zucchini Rounds

          Fresh zucchini, cut in rounds
          Real butter
          Grated Parmesan cheese
          Salt and pepper to taste

Melt butter on griddle or in frying pan. Fry zucchini until cooked through. Sprinkle with Parmesan, and salt and pepper. Drain on paper towels. Serve hot.

Cheese Toast Canapes

6   slices white bread
4   green onions, chopped
4   large sprigs of parsley, chopped
¾   cup grated Cheddar
½   cup real mayonnaise

Toast 12 slices of white bread on one side only in broiler. Cut off crusts. Combine remaining ingredients in a bowl. Spread mixture on untoasted side of bread. Broil 'til bubbly.
    These may be frozen (uncooked).

Variation: Add sauteed mushrooms and/or crabmeat.

Mexican Pinwheels

4   ounces cream cheese, softened
⅔   cup grated Cheddar cheese
4   tablespoons chopped green chilis
4   tablespoons chopped black olives
2   teaspoons chopped onion
7   drops tabasco sauce
1   tube crescent roll mix

Combine all ingredients except the crescent rolls. Open tube of rolls and separate into four rectangles. Press perforations to seal dough. Spread ¼ of the cheese mixture over each rectangle. Roll rectangles starting from the short end. Cut each roll into ten slices. Place pinwheels, cut side down, onto greased cookie sheet or foil lined cookie sheet.
    Bake at 375° 12-15 minutes.

Chili-Cheese Squares

½   cup butter
10   eggs
½   cup flour
1   teaspoon baking powder
     dash of salt
7   ounce can diced green chilis
1   pint small curd cottage cheese
½   pound Monterey Jack cheese, grated
½   pound grated Cheddar cheese

Melt the butter in a 13"x9"x2" pan. In a large bowl lightly beat the eggs. Add flour, baking powder, and salt. Mix well.

Add the melted butter from the baking dish, the chilis, cottage cheese, Cheddar cheese and Monterey Jack cheese. Stir until blended. Pour into buttered baking dish.

Bake 15 minutes at 400°. Reduce temperature to 350° and bake an additional 35-45 minutes or until center is firm. Cool slightly. Cut into squares. Serve warm.

Petite Quiches

Quiche Lorraine

        *Cream cheese pastry (page 88)
¾   cup half and half or heavy cream
2   eggs, slightly beaten
¼   teaspoon salt
1   cup firmly packed Natural Swiss cheese grated
1   tablespoon flour
4   slices bacon cooked crisp and crumbled

Mix cream, eggs and salt. Toss cheese and flour, then add to egg mixture. Fold in bacon. Pour two-thirds full into miniature muffin pans lined with pastry. Bake at 325° for 30-35 minutes. May be frozen after baking. Yields: 48.

*For large parties double the pastry and roll into a jelly roll pan. Then double your quiche filling. Pour filling into jelly roll pan. After baking cut into squares.

Zucchini Quiche

Cream cheese pastry (page 88)
¼ cup grated parmesan
½ cup grated Gruyere or Swiss cheese
*2 cups grated zucchini (2 medium)
1⅓ cups heavy cream
4 eggs
½ teaspoon salt
1/8 teaspoon nutmeg
1/8 teaspoon pepper
1 tablespoon butter

Layer zucchini and cheeses over crust. Whisk together cream, eggs and salt, nutmeg and pepper. Pour over zucchini and cheese. Dot with butter. Bake at 350° for 30-40 minutes or until set.

If using a jelly roll pan, double the recipe.

*One package frozen chopped spinach defrosted and squeezed may be substituted for zucchini.

This may be frozen.

Avocado-Crab Quiche

	cream cheese pastry (page 88)
2	fresh avocados, cut into small chunks
1	tablespoon lemon juice
½	teaspoon salt
12	ounces of chunk crabmeat
	dash of tabasco
4	eggs
1½	cups heavy cream
¼	cup dry white wine
	pinch of salt
	fresh ground pepper
	pinch of nutmeg
1	cup Monterey Jack cheese grated

Toss avocado in lemon juice and salt. Place a piece of avocado in each petite muffin pan lined with pastry. Mix tabasco and crabmeat. Place crab with avocado in each cup. Sprinkle with grated Monterey Jack cheese.

With wire whisk beat the eggs, cream, wine, salt, pepper and nutmeg. Pour custard over cheese.

Bake at 325° 30 minutes or until browned.

Stuffers For Cherry Tomatoes

Curried Tuna

¼   cup real mayonnaise
¼   cup sour cream
1   tablespoon lemon juice
½   teaspoon salt
½   teaspoon curry powder
2   hard boiled eggs, chopped
1   teaspoon grated onion
½   can water chestnuts, chopped
5   green olives chopped
1   teaspoon small capers
1   7-ounce can tuna fish, drained
2   boxes cherry tomatoes
    fresh parsley for garnish

Combine mayonnaise and sour cream. Add lemon juice, salt and curry. Mix well. Fold in eggs, onion, water chestnuts, olives and capers. Mix with tuna. Stuff in hollowed out cherry tomatoes. Garnish with parsley.

Shrimp Filling
For Cherry Tomatoes

1   can baby shrimp, drained
½   cup mayonnaise
1   stalk celery, chopped fine
    salt and pepper to taste
2   hard boiled eggs, chopped

Combine ingredients. Stuff tomatoes. Garnish with parsley.

Asparagus Rolls

1	8-ounce package cream cheese
1	4-ounce package Kraft Blue Cheese
1	egg
1	loaf Arnolds Very Thin White Bread or regular white white bread rolled thin with a rolling pin
1	can green asparagus spears or 1 medium bunch fresh asparagus cooked until tender and drained
½	cup melted butter

Cut crusts from bread. With electric mixer blend cream cheese, Blue cheese and egg. Spread mixture on bread. Roll around the asparagus. Cut in three pieces. (Asparagus Rolls may be frozen at this point. Place on cookie sheet. Freeze. Then put in plastic bags.) Just before baking, brush lightly with melted butter. Bake at 350° 20-30 minutes. Serve hot. Yields: 57 appetizers.

Bacon-Cheese Toast Canapes

8	slices bacon, cooked drained and crumbled
½	pound sharp Cheddar, grated
	small onion, chopped
1	tablespoon dry mustard
	few drops worcestershire
1	tablespoon mayonnaise

Combine ingredients. Spread on party rye bread slices. Broil 'til bubbly. May be frozen after spread on bread.

Spear it With
a Toothpick

Artichokes In Blue Cheese

3 packages frozen artichoke hearts or 3-8 ½
  ounce cans artichoke hearts
1 stick butter
6 ounces Kraft Blue cheese

Defrost artichokes and drain well. Cut each artichoke in half. Melt butter and cheese together. Combine cheese, butter and artichokes and transfer to chafing dish. Spear with a toothpick!

Bacon Wraps

1 can water chestnuts
1 pound bacon
1 cup sherry

Slice water chestnuts in thirds. Cook bacon partially, but it must be soft. Roll water chestnuts in bacon strips and spear with a toothpick. Marinate in sherry for several hours. Place marinated bacon-chestnuts under broiler and cook until bacon is crisp.

Olive Wraps

Wrap large green olives stuffed with pimentos in ½ slice of bacon. Spear with a toothpick. Broil on one side. Drain. Turn over. Broil on other side until bacon is crisp. Serve hot.

Mexican Meatballs

1	pound ground chuck
1	egg, beaten
¾·1	cup fine bread crumbs
4	ounces green chili salsa (page 89)
3	tablespoons (or more) diced green chilis
2	tablespoons worcestershire sauce
½	teaspoon M.S.G. (optional)
½	teaspoon garlic powder
1	can pitted ripe olives
½	cup grated Parmesan
4	tablespoons sesame seeds

Mix the first eight ingredients together. Form into 1 inch balls, stuffing each with an olive. (Another way to do this is to chop your olives in a food processor and mix in with meat mixture.) Mix Parmesan and sesame seeds. Roll meatballs in mixture. Place coated meatballs on cookie sheets and bake at 350° 12-15 minutes.

Spinach Chicken
With Oriental Dip

    4   large chicken breasts that have been boned and
            skinned
    1   can chicken broth
    ¼   cup soy sauce
    1   tablespoon worcestershire
    1   bag fresh spinach

Cook chicken breasts in broth, soy sauce and worcestershire until fork tender. Cool in broth. Cut chicken into bite size chunks. Wash spinach thoroughly and place leaves in colander. Pour about two quarts of boiling water over leaves. Drain and cool. Roll chicken cubes in spinach leaves. Secure with toothpicks. Chill thoroughly.

Oriental Dip:

    1   cup sour cream
    2   teaspoons sesame seeds
    ½   teaspoon ground ginger
    4   teaspoons soy sauce
    2   teaspoons worcestershire

Mix well. Chill overnight to season. Place in small bowl next to speared chicken.

This recipe is best if prepared the day before serving.

Hawaiian Sausage Balls

½   pound pork sausage
¾   pound ground pork
½   teaspoon salt
½   teaspoon dry mustard
¼   teaspoon ground allspice
1   egg, lightly beaten
¼   cup fine bread crumbs
2   green onions, chopped
½   cup apple jelly
½   cup chopped chutney
1   teaspoon lemon juice

In a bowl, stir sausage, pork, salt, mustard, allspice, egg, bread crumbs and onion. Blend well. Shape into 1 inch balls. (At this point you may freeze these.)

Place thawed meatballs on cookie sheets and bake at 350° for 10-12 minutes or until well browned. Drain. In a large frying pan, over low heat, stir in apple jelly, chutney and lemon juice. Stir until jelly is melted. Add meatballs. Simmer 8-10 minutes. Transfer to chafing dish.

Celery Victor

3 bunches celery hearts
2 cups chicken broth
¼ cup fresh parsley
1 bay leaf

Cut the celery to desired lengths, short for hors d'oeuvre and salads, longer for individual appetizers. Boil, then simmer 'til tender in a saucepan containing the broth, parsley and bay leaf. Cool in broth. Remove when cool and marinate overnight in the following mixture:

6 tablespoons red wine vinegar
1 tablespoon Dijon mustard
1 cup of corn oil
1 teaspoon salt
1 teaspoon pepper

Remove from marinade.
Garnish with parsley and pimentos.

Supreme Sausages

5 ounces red currant jelly
5 ounces apple jelly
5 ounces prepared French's mustard
2 packages Oscar Mayer Smokey Sausages
(little smokies) or any good smoked
sausage cut in bite size chunks

Combine jellies and mustard. Heat through. Add sausages. Serve in chafing dish.

Korean Beef With Vegetables

2	pounds beef sirloin, 1 inch thick
6	tablespoons sesame oil
¾	cup soy sauce
3-6	garlic cloves, mashed
1	tablespoon vinegar
1/8	teaspoon pepper
2	tablespoons sesame seeds
1	teaspoon sugar
1	large onion, cut in large strips
1	large green pepper, cut into bite size pieces
1	zucchini, cut in bite size pieces

In a bowl stir together sesame oil, soy sauce, garlic, vinegar, pepper, sesame seeds and sugar. Marinate steak, onion, green pepper and zucchini in a covered container for at least 4 hours. Take steak out of marinade and cut into bite size cubes.

Saute beef in a little oil. In same oil saute green peppers, onions and zucchini. Transfer meat and vegetables to chafing dish. Add some marinade. Serve hot. Spear with toothpicks.

Optional: Add cherry tomatoes.

Stuffed Mushrooms

The following recipes are great for
broiled mushroom caps — fresh mushrooms, of course.

Bacon-Cheese Mushrooms

4	slices cooked bacon, crumbled
1	small onion chopped
½	cup grated Parmesan cheese
½	teaspoon worcestershire
¼	cup bread crumbs
¼	cup chopped black olives
1	pound fresh mushrooms

Combine first six ingredients. Mix well. Stuff into cleaned mushroom caps. Broil until bubbly. Serve hot.

Cheese-Nut Mushrooms

4	ounces Kraft Blue Cheese
4	ounces walnut pieces
2	tablespoons melted butter
1	pound fresh mushrooms

Mix together Blue cheese, nuts and butter. Stuff in mushroom caps. Broil until bubbly. Serve hot.

Oriental Mushrooms

6   tablespoons butter, melted
2   cloves garlic, mashed
½   pound Monterey Jack cheese, grated
4   tablespoons dry white wine
2   teaspoons soy sauce
6   tablespoons cracker crumbs
1   pound fresh mushrooms

Combine first six ingredients. Mix well. Stuff in mushroom caps. Broil until bubbly. Serve hot.

Blue-Pecan Mushrooms

8   ounces cream cheese, softened
4   ounce package Kraft Blue Cheese
2   tablespoons milk
¼   cup choppped onion
½   cup finely chopped pecans
1   pound fresh mushrooms

Cream cheeses together. Mix in milk, onion and pecans. Stuff in mushroom caps. Broil until bubbly. Serve hot.

Bacon-Mushroom Wraps

1   loaf thin sandwich bread (white)
1   can cream of mushroom soup
1   pound bacon

Decrust bread and cut into three strips. Spread undiluted soup on one side of the bread strips. Cut uncooked bacon strips in half. Place bread strips, soup side up, on the bacon strips and roll (bacon is the outer layer). Place in a baking dish. Bake at 300° for 1 hour.

Marinated Mushrooms

⅔   cup red wine vinegar
½   cup salad oil
1   clove garlic, mashed
1½   tablespoons sugar
1   teaspoon salt
2   teaspoons tarragon
4   drops tabasco
1   bay leaf
1   teaspoon marjoram
1   onion sliced into rings
1   pound fresh bite size mushrooms

Combine ingredients. Refrigerate for several hours, or overnight. Drain before serving.

Hors D'oeuvre de Mer

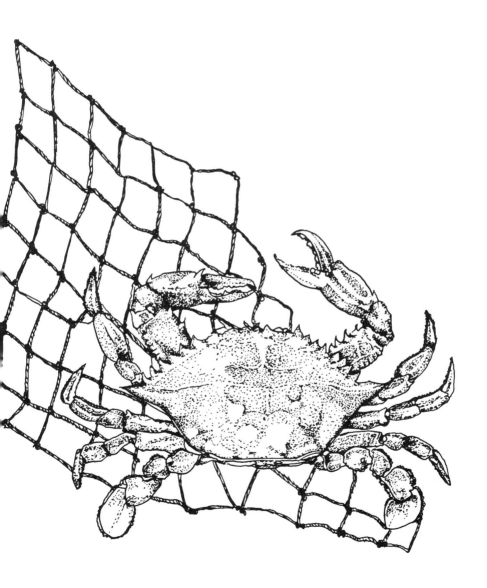

Mornay Sauce For Crab Claws And Large Shrimp

½	stick of butter
⅓	cup of flour
2	cups of heavy cream, heated
1	cup of chicken broth, heated
½	cup of clam juice
¼	cup of medium sherry
¼	cup of dry white wine
½	teaspoon lemon juice
	pinch of nutmeg
1½	cups grated Monterey Jack cheese
	Fresh crab claws
	Fresh large shrimp, peeled and cooked

In a saucepan melt butter. With a wire whisk stir in flour, stirring to make a roux (paste). Cook for two minutes. Remove from heat. Again using a wire whisk stir in two cups of heavy cream and 1 cup of chicken broth, both of which have been heated. Return to heat and cook until thickened.

Add clam juice, sherry, white wine and lemon juice and then nutmeg. Heat thoroughly. Add grated cheese. Stir until smooth.

Place in chafing dish and serve with mounds of crab claws and large cooked shrimp. Alongside also have a bowl of cocktail sauce (a mixture of ketchup and horseradish to taste).

Sour Dough Shrimp Dip

1   round loaf Sour Dough Bread
6   cups grated Cheddar cheese
⅓   cup flour
1   small can baby shrimp, drained and chopped
1   can cream of shrimp soup
⅔   cup sour cream
1   clove garlic, mashed
¼   teaspoon cayenne pepper
¼   cup dry white wine
     raw vegetables and bread cubes for dippers

Slice off top of load of bread. Remove the soft center and cut into 1" cubes. In a sauce pan, mix cheese, flour, soup, shrimp, sour cream, garlic, cayenne, and white wine. Heat over medium heat until smooth. Let stand ten minutes to thicken.

Pour into sourdough bread shell. Serve with vegetable and bread dippers.

Crab And
Water Chestnut Spread

1   pound crab, flaked
1   small can water chestnuts, chopped
2   tablespoons soy sauce
½   cup mayonnaise
2   tablespoons chopped green onions

Mix ingredients. Refrigerate until chilled. Serve on Triscuits.

Crabmeat Cocktail Block

8 ounces of cream cheese, softened
¼ cup real mayonnaise
1 tablespoon chopped onion
8 ounces of flaked crabmeat
⅔ cup ketchup
1-3 tablespoons of horseradish

Blend cream cheese, mayonnaise and onion. Spread into a small serving dish. Mix ketchup and horseradish. Spread on top of cream cheese mixture. Top with flaked crabmeat. Serve with crackers.

Crab-Artichoke-Mushroom Appetizer

A marvelous first course for a dinner party. Presented best when served in small shell plates.

8	ounces of chunks of King Crab meat
1	can artichoke hearts, or fresh artichoke hearts
½	pound fresh mushrooms, sliced
3	tablespoons of butter
3	tablespoons of flour
1½	cups of milk
1	teaspoon worcestershire
¼	cup cream sherry
½	teaspoon salt
	dash pepper
	grated Parmesan cheese
	paprika and fresh parsley for garnish

Saute mushrooms in oil until tender. Season with garlic powder. Drain.

In saucepan melt butter and add flour. Stir with whisk making a roux (paste). Slowly add milk and cook until thickened. Blend in worcestershire, sherry, salt and pepper. Place crab, artichokes, and mushrooms in each shell. Top with sauce. Sprinkle with Parmesan.

Bake at 350° 12-15 minutes. Place on plates with paper doilies. Garnish with paprika and parsley.

Shrimp Or Crab Mold

8   ounces of cream cheese
8   ounces (or more) baby shrimp or flaked
    crabmeat
1   small onion, chopped
1   cup chopped celery
1   cup real mayonnaise
1   can cream of mushroom soup
1   package of Knox gelatin
2   tablespoons cold water

Heat soup in double boiler. Dissolve gelatin in cold water. Add to soup and mix well. Cool slightly and fold in remaining ingredients. Chill in refrigerator several hours until firm. Serve with crackers.

Avocado Crab Dip

3   medium avocados
½   cup sour cream
1   can crabmeat, drained and flaked
½   teaspoon lemon juice
1   teaspoon horseradish
    garlic powder to taste
    salt and pepper to taste
3   tablespoons green chili salsa

Mash avocados. Combine all ingredients. Spread on crackers.

Pink Shrimp Mousse

1	can tomato soup
8	ounces cream cheese
2	envelopes Knox unflavored gelatin
½	cup cold water
1	cup of real mayonnaise
¾	cup of chopped celery
¾	cup chopped onion
2-4	cans of baby shrimp

In a double boiler heat soup and add cut up cream cheese. Stir with wire whisk until well blended. Mix 2 envelopes of gelatin to ½ cup cold water and add to soup mixture. Let cool slightly. Fold in mayonnaise, celery, onion and shrimp. Pour into a greased fancy mold. Chill several hours until firm. Serve with Ritz crackers.

Salmon Party Log

1	pound can of red or pink salmon
1	tablespoon lemon juice
8	ounces cream cheese
2	teaspoons grated onion
1	teaspoon horseradish
¼	teaspoon salt
¼	teaspoon liquid smoke
¾	cup chopped pecans
¼	cup snipped parsley

Drain and flake salmon, removing skin and bones. Combine salmon with lemon juice, cream cheese, onion, horseradish, salt and liquid smoke. Mix thoroughly. Roll into log. Smother with pecans and parsley. Chill until firm. Serve with Ritz and other crackers.

Hot Cheese-Crab

10   ounces Cracker Barrel Natural Sharp
      Cheddar Cheese
8   ounces Kraft Olde English Sharp Process
      American Cheese
⅓   cup milk
⅓   cup white wine
6-8 ounces flaked crab meat

Dice or shred cheese and cook over low heat with milk until blended well. Stir in wine and crab. Heat through. Serve with Triscuits and other favorite crackers.

Clam Dip For Potato Chips

8   ounces of cream cheese, softened
2   tablespoons of clam juice
1   clove of garlic, mashed
1-2 green onions, chopped
2   tablespoons mayonnaise
1   teaspoon worcestershire
1   teaspoon anchovy paste
1   can minced clams, drained

With electric mixer whip the cream cheese with the clam juice, mayonnaise and worcestershire. Fold in garlic, onions, anchovy paste and clams. Taste for seasoning. Refrigerate 3-4 hours. Serve with potato chips.

Crab-Clam Spread

The ultimate of seafood spreads!

8   ounces of cream cheese
½   cup real mayonnaise
2   green onions, chopped
1   tablespoon fresh parsley, chopped
1   6-ounce can of crabmeat, drained and
     flaked
1   6-ounce can of minced clams, drained
½   cup of sliced almonds
1   tablespoon of horseradish
¼   teaspoon worcestershire
2   tablespoons dry white wine

In a bowl combine all ingredients. Place in a square baking dish. Heat through (350° 15-20 minutes). Serve with Ritz crackers.

Note: May be served in chafing dish.

King Crab Spread

6-8 ounces King Crab Meat
2   tablespoons butter
¼   cup chopped green onions
1   cup chopped mushrooms
1   cup shredded Monterey Jack cheese
1-3 ounce package of cream cheese
⅓   cup mayonnaise
2   tablespoons chopped parsley
1   teaspoon horseradish
½   teaspoon worcestershire

Sauté mushrooms and onions in butter for 2-3 minutes. Combine with remaining ingredients. Place in small ovenproof dish.
Bake at 350° for 20 minutes, 'til heated through. Serve with crackers or French bread rounds.

Fruits De Mer

¾   pound lump crabmeat
¾   pound medium shrimp, deshelled and
       deveined
       butter
1   shallot or green onion, chopped
¼   cup tarragon vinegar
¼   teaspoon dry mustard
½   cup sour cream, room temperature
       fresh mushrooms, sliced
¼   cup Italian flavored breadcrumbs

In a skillet, melt 2 tablespoons butter and saute onion and mushrooms. Remove from heat and drain. In a bowl mix vinegar, mustard and sour cream. Fold in seafood and mushroom-onion mixture. Spoon into ramekins or shell dishes. Sprinkle with bread crumbs and dot with butter.

Bake at 350° 15 minutes or until bubbly. Garnish with parsley.

Oysters Bluepoint

An Eastern Shore specialty
that turned Nonnie into an oyster fan!

1   quart fresh or canned oysters, drained
1   stick butter
1   teaspoon pepper
       dash tabasco sauce
1   tablespoon Beau Monde Seasoning (Spice
       Islands)

Make a sauce with the last 4 ingredients.

Cook oysters in sauce until edges curl. Do not overcook, as oysters will become tough. If sauce becomes too thin after cooking add more butter. Transfer to chafing dish, juice and all. Garnish with snipped parsley. Spear with long pics.

Parmesan-Garlic Shrimp

20	fresh shrimp, medium sized
¼	cup olive oil
	bread crumbs
½	teaspoon crushed red peppers
2-4	large garlic cloves, mashed
¼	cup fresh chopped parsley
6	tablespoons fresh butter, melted
¼-½	cup grated Parmesan

Preheat oven to 300°.

Shell and devein shrimp. Pat dry. Arrange in oiled pan. Pour olive oil over shrimp. Then sprinkle with a light layer of bread crumbs followed by salt, pepper and red peppers. Top with garlic and parsley.

Cover with foil and bake for 15 minutes. Remove from oven -turn shrimp over. Spoon butter over shrimp and sprinkle with Parmesan.

Bake uncovered another 5 minutes or until shrimp have turned completely white. Serve hot.

Seviche

1   *pound raw small scallops*
1   *pound raw red snapper*
1   *pound medium shrimp shelled and cooked*
1   *cup lime juice freshly squeezed*
6   *tablespoons red onion, chopped*
4   *tablespoons fresh parsley, chopped*
4   *tablespoons chopped green chilis*
½   *cup safflower oil*
¾   *teaspoon dried oregano*
     dash of tabasco
1   *teaspoon salt*
1/8 *teaspoon ground pepper*
2   *fresh avocados*

Add lime juice to scallops, red snapper and shrimp. Marinate 3-4 hours in refrigerator, covered. Drain and discard juice. Toss gently with onion, parsley, chilis, oil, oregano, tabasco, salt, and pepper.

Chill for at least an hour. Place in serving bowl and garnish with fresh parsley sprigs and small wedges of avocado. Spear with pics.

Spur of
The Moment
Hors D'oeuvres

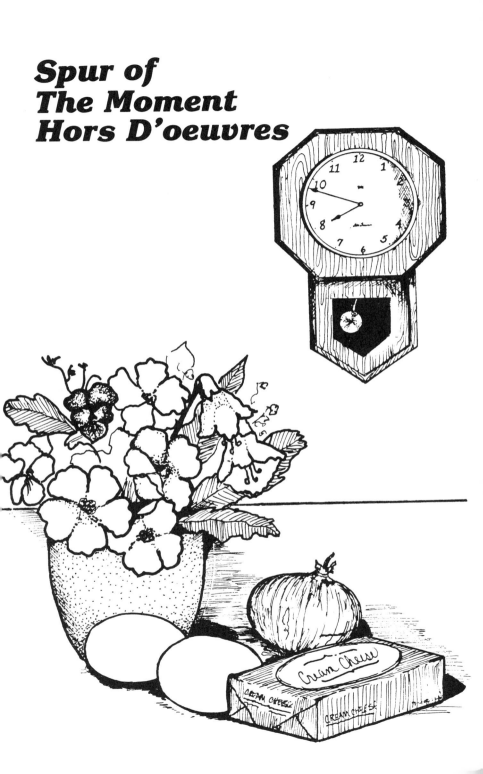

Salami — Onion Rolls

slices of salami
cream cheese
fresh green onions

Smear salami with cream cheese. Place a fresh green onion on cream cheese. Roll salami around the onion. Cut into 1" pieces. Secure with toothpicks.

Ham Pinwheels

sliced boiled ham
cream cheese, softened

Spread softened cream cheese on sliced boiled ham. Roll. Cut into pinwheels.

Sherried Dates

16 ounce package pitted dates
1 cup cream sherry
pecan halves

Marinate dates in sherry for one day in the refrigerator. Remove dates from sherry, stuffing each with a pecan half. Store in air tight container up to one month.

Another quick-to-fix date treat is to simply stuff pitted dates with a small chunk of cream cheese. Spear with pics.

Party Mix

A homemade blend that can be frozen for a quick snack!

6 tablespoons butter
1 teaspoon Lawry's seasoned salt
4 teaspoons worcestershire
2 cups Corn Chex cereal
2 cups Rice Chex cereal
2 cups Wheat Chex cereal
2 cups very thin pretzel sticks
1-2 cups whole mixed nuts

Melt butter in a jelly roll pan in a 250° oven. Stir in seasoned salt and worcestershire. Add Chex and pretzels and nuts, stirring well. Heat about 30 minutes, stirring occasionally. Spread on paper towels. Freeze in airtight container until ready to use.

Holiday idea: Place in jars with decorated tops for holiday gifts!

Easy Escargots

So easy and so delicious,
but make sure your guests like the French delicacy

1 7-ounce can escargots, drained well
1 stick real butter
fresh parsley, chopped
fresh garlic cloves
French bread cut in slices then quartered
Optional: a dash of brandy

Melt butter in small pan. Add fresh parsley and garlic to taste. Add drained escargots. Heat through. Serve heated. Spoon on to small slices of French bread.

Bricks Of Cream Cheese

How they can come to your rescue
for a quick, tasty hors d'oeuvre

Top a brick of cream cheese with one of the following:

Barbeque sauce (Open Pit is great)
Hot Pepper Jelly
Chutney
Caviar — Red or Black
Picapeppa Sauce (Jamaican)

Spread on your favorite cracker and enjoy.

Susan's Zucchini Snacks

- Cut fresh zucchini into bite size strips or chunks
- Squeeze fresh lemon to coat lightly
- Sprinkle with pepper
- Serve alone or with cheese wedges and crackers

The Sweet
Part of
The Party

Amaretto Fondue

3 ounce package vanilla pudding (not instant)
1 cup whole milk
  Cool Whip or fresh whipped cream to taste
  Amaretto to taste (start with ¼ cup)

Cook each 3 ounces of pudding with 1 cup of milk, stirring until thickened. Cover. Cool to room temperature.

With wire whisk stir in Cool Whip or whipped fresh cream and Amaretto — to taste. Dip with bananas, honeydew, canteloupe, fresh strawberries, etc.

Serve at room temperature. Use bamboo skewers for dipping.

For an elegant dessert, layer fruits in parfait glasses and top with fondue.

Chocolate Fondue

The easiest and best tasting fondue comes in a 1 pound can: Hershey's Chocolate Fudge Topping. Heat in chafing dish or electric fondue pot. Dip with fresh fruits — bananas and strawberries a must.

Fruit Boat

Using a ripe watermelon, carve out the fruit, designing a boat or basket. Deseed the watermelon, cutting the fruit into chunks or balls. Do the same with honeydews, cantaloupes and papaya. Salvage all the juice from the fruits you use. Cut cleaned strawberries, oranges, apples, bananas, etc.

To natural juices, add Gran Marnier liqueur and brandy to taste. If you do not have enough juice add orange juice. Pour juices over cut fruits in watermelon shell. Spear with party pics.

Petite Pecan Tarts

Prepare pastry (page 88)

Filling for pecan tarts:

¼   *pound butter*
2   *egg yolks, beaten*
2   *cups chopped pecans*
2   *egg whites, beaten stiff*
1   *cup sugar*
½   *teaspoon vanilla*

Cream sugar and butter. Add the egg yolks, vanilla and pecans. Mix well. Fold in egg whites. Fill small muffin pans which have been lined with pastry.
Bake 20 minutes at 350°.
Keep pastry dough thin. This recipe can make 48 small tarts. Can be frozen after baking.

Caramel Brownies

⅓   *cup evaporated milk*
1   *package German chocolate cake mix*
¾   *cup melted butter*
⅓   *cup evaporated milk*
1   *14-ounce package Kraft vanilla caramels*
6   *ounces chocolate chips*

Mix 1st 3 ingredients and spread one-half of the mixture into a greased 9"x13" pan. Bake at 350° 6 minutes. Melt a 14-ounce package Kraft vanilla caramels with another ⅓ cup evaporated milk. Drizzle onto baked layer. Sprinkle with 6 ounces of chocolate chips and then top with remaining cake mixture.
Bake 18 minutes. Cool before cutting. Refrigerate. These can be frozen but they are so good they won't last long!

Cheesecake Squares

Crust:

    1 ¼   *cup graham cracker crumbs*
    ¼   *cup melted butter*

Filling:

    3   *8-ounce packages cream cheese*
    1   *cup sugar*
    5   *eggs*
    1 ½   *teaspoons vanilla*

Combine crust ingredients thoroughly. Pat into 13"x9" pan.
Cream cheese and sugar thoroughly. Add eggs one at a time and add vanilla. Pour over graham cracker crust.
Bake at 325° for 40 minutes.

Topping:

    1   *pint sour cream*
    4   *tablespoons sugar*
    1   *teaspoon vanilla*

Pour topping over baked portion, return to oven at 475° for 5 minutes. Cut into one inch squares while still hot. Refrigerate 'til well chilled.

Almond Roca

Great for holiday gifts!

1   cup sugar
1   cup real butter
1   large Hershey Almond Bar
1   small bag slivered almonds

Break up candy bar into small pieces and spread into an 8"x8" square pan. Sprinkle with almonds. Cook butter and sugar stirring together until the color of Kraft Caramel. Spread mixture evenly over chocolate and almonds. Allow to cool. Break out of dish with a stiff knife.

Tips: DO NOT BUTTER DISH — DO NOT DOUBLE RECIPES

Individually wrap pieces with decorative foil.

Peanut Butter Chocolate Bars

12 graham crackers, crushed
1   cup melted butter
1   cup peanut butter
1   pound powdered sugar
2   8-ounce Hershey's Milk Chocolate Bars
1   cup (or more) chopped nuts

Combine crackers, butter, peanut butter, and sugar. Mix well. Pat into a jelly roll pan.

Melt 2 large Hershey's Milk Chocolate Bars (8 ounces each) and pour over crust. Top with chopped nuts. Let stand at room temperature one hour. Cut and refrigerate 24 hours. These can also be frozen.

Peppermint Brownies

Brownies:

½	cup butter
1	cup sugar
2	eggs
½	cup cocoa
½	cup flour
½	teaspoon vanilla

Cream together butter and sugar. Add eggs. Blend in cocoa and flour. Then add vanilla. Mix well. Pour into an 8" square pan, greased.
Bake at 350° for 30-35 minutes. Cool completely.

Frosting:

1½	cups confectioners sugar
4	tablespoons butter
1	teaspoon milk
½	teaspoon peppermint extract

Beat ingredients until smooth. Spread over brownies.

Glaze:

2	tablespoons butter
2	squares unsweetened chocolate

Melt butter and chocolate over low heat. Blend well. Dribble over frosting. Serve cold.

Pineapple Fluff Dip

1   fresh pineapple
1   7-ounce jar marshmallow fluff
4   ounces cream cheese, softened

   Cut off outer skin of pineapple and cut out the inner core. Cut pineapple into bite size chunks. With a wire whisk mix the marshmallow and cream cheese. Arrange the pineapple around a bowl of the dip and serve with pics for dipping.

Variation: Marinate the pineapple in creme de menthe before serving.

Chocolate Cups

12   ounces of chocolate chips
      paper muffin cup liners, or small paper
       candy liners
      Amaretto Fondue or favorite cordial

   In double boiler melt chocolate chips. Paint chocolate on the inside of the paper liners. Chill until firm. Remove paper. Fill cups with Amaretto Fondue, or after dinner drinks (small cups only).

Brownie Mounds

3⅓	cups flour
1	teaspoon baking powder
½	teaspoon salt
⅔	cup margarine, softened
1½	cups sugar
⅔	cup Karo light corn syrup
2	eggs
6	1-ounce squares of unsweetened chocolate, melted
2	teaspoons vanilla
1½	cups coarsely choppped walnuts

Sift together flour, baking powder and salt. In another bowl mix margarine, and sugar. Stir in corn syrup, and eggs. Blend well. Stir in remaining ingredients. Drop by heaping tablespoonsful onto greased baking sheets.

Bake at 350° 10-12 minutes. Yields: 4 dozen. These freeze beautifully.

Apricot Squares

1   cup sifted flour
1   stick butter, cut into small pieces
⅓   cup sugar
⅔   cup dried apricots
2   eggs
1   cup dark brown sugar
⅓   cup flour
½   teaspoon baking powder
¼   teaspoon salt
1   cup chopped walnuts
½   teaspoon vanilla
½   cup confectioners sugar

In a bowl combine flour, butter and sugar. Mixture will be crumbly. Press into an 8'" square pan. Bake at 350° for 25-30 minutes or until lightly browned.

In a saucepan boil dried apricots covered with water for 10 minutes. Drain and cool. Chop cooled apricots in food processor using steel blade. Then add (in food processor) eggs, brown sugar, and a mixture of flour, baking powder and salt. Transfer to mixing bowl and fold in 1 cup chopped walnuts and ½ teaspoon vanilla. Spread mixture over baked layer.

Bake at 350° for 30-40 minutes. Let cool. Sprinkle with confectioners sugar. Cut into squares.

Strawberry Fundue!

1   pint of bite size strawberries
1   cup sour cream
1   cup brown sugar (regular or granulated)

Wash strawberries and remove stems. Place strawberries in a bowl next to a small bowl of brown sugar and a small bowl of sour cream. With party pics spear strawberries, dip in sour cream then in brown sugar . . . then to your mouth . . . delicious! Can be presented in a Lazy Susan.

Miscellaneous

Cream Cheese Pastry Crust

    3   ounces cream cheese
    1   stick of butter
 1 ½   cups flour

Cream butter and cream cheese. Add flour. Mix well. Form into a ball and chill well. Chill covered for 1-3 hours in refrigerator. Roll dough out. If rolled thin, recipe can yield 48 miniature shells.

Sweet And Sour Sauce

When you serve the Pork-Shrimp Lumpia (page 39), plan to have a ham for the same party. Coat a 10 pound fresh ham with a 1 pound can of crushed pineapple and 1 pound box of light brown sugar. Bake until heated through. Remove ham from pan, scraping off the pineapple-sugar coating. Serve ham warm or room temperature with small Parkerhouse rolls or biscuits.

Place the pineapple-sugar mixture in an electric blender and whirl until well blended. This makes an excellent sauce for lumpia!

Green Chili Salsa

A main ingredient in many
of the recipes throughout this book

20 medium, fresh tomatoes
1 medium onion, chopped
5-15 chopped fresh jalopenia peppers (5 for
  mild, 10 for medium, 15 for hot)
1 tablespoon salt

Pour boiling water over tomatoes and let stand for about a minute. Skin will peel off easily. Cut tomatoes into chunks and place in large pot. Add chopped onion and peppers. Stir well. Bring to a boil then simmer uncovered about 20 minutes, stirring often. Add salt.

Boil 12 half-pint jars, or sterilize them in the dishwasher. Boil lids, bands and large dipping spoon. If salsa is too watery spoon off some liquid. Pour hot salsa into sterilized jars. Seal tight. Set aside. Lids will"pop' to indicate that it has sealed.

*Above is the homemade recipe for green chili salsa. It is great to have on hand for many recipes and for hostess gifts. You can also buy salsa in most grocery stores either in the gourmet section or Mexican/Spanish food section. Here are different brand names:

Ortega Green Chili Salsa
Old El Paso Tomatoes and Green Chilis
La Victoria Salsa Ranchera
Ashley's of Texas
RO-tel Tomatoes & Green Chilis

Party Planning

Guidelines For Party Planning

1) Have an occasion and plan ahead as far as possible.

2) Send invitations 2-3 weeks before the party.

3) BE ENTHUSIASTIC

4) Plan menu, appropriate for the occasion.

5) Make shopping lists.

6) Make checklists.

7) Start cooking ahead of time and freeze as much as possible.

8) Allow time for house preparation.
   a) Set up bar several days ahead of time.
   b) Plan to have food in every possible room. Put notes where you plan to place food.
   c) Have an attractive main table with flowers or holiday decorations.
   d) Have ashtrays available in every room, including the bathroom.
   e) Have bathrooms in order with an ample supply of guest towels and toilet paper.
   f) Have lots of clean dishtowels for the kitchen and bar.

9) Try to leave the day of the party open for party preparation only.

10) Use checklists.

11) Again, BE ENTHUSIASTIC!

Keep a record of guests and menu.

Record special notes — favorite recipes, things you could do differently; and remember, mistakes are learning experiences.

IMPORTANT — Enjoy your own party!

Party Planner Menus

6-10 people before theatre:

Artichoke Heart Cheese Dip with Tortilla chips
**Colorful Mexican Dip with Tortilla chips
*Mexican Meatballs

6-10 people before dinner:

**Dill Dip with fresh vegetables
*Hawaiian Sausage Balls

10-20 people before theatre:

Crab-Clam Spread with crackers
**Hot Chipped Beef Spread with Triscuits
*Zucchini Squares (double batch)
**Supreme Sausages

10-20 people before dinner:

Artichoke-Crab-Mushroom Appetizer served in shell plates
Mango-Chutney Cheese pate with crackers

*FREEZABLE

**CAN BE PREPARED AT LEAST TWO DAYS AHEAD

6-10 people for afternoon cocktails:

**Hormel Chili Cheese Dip with tortilla chips
  Guacamole with tortilla chips
**Curry Dip with vegetables
  Supreme Sausages
  Strawberry Fondue
 *Brownie Mounds

10-25 people for afternoon cocktails:

  Broccoli-Mushroom-Cheese Dip with Tortilla chips
**Hot Bean Dip with Tortilla chips
**Salmon Party Log with crackers
 *Artichoke Cheese Squares
 *Zucchini Bars
  Amaretto Fondue
 *Caramel Brownies

10-30 people for an evening cocktail party

**Chili Con Quesa with tortilla chips
**Hot Bean Dip with tortilla chips
 *Mexican Meatballs
**Cheese'n Chutney Ball
  Crabmeat Cocktail Block
 *Curried Mushroom Rolls
  Oysters Bluepoint
  Fruitboat
 *Petite Pecan Tarts

 *FREEZABLE

**CAN BE PREPARED AT LEAST TWO DAYS AHEAD

30-60 people for an evening cocktail party

**Swiss Cheese Dip with raw vegetables
**Salmon Party Log with crackers
  Ham with small rolls
 *Lumpia with sauces
**Frito-Bean Beef Dip with tortilla chips
  Petite Avocado-Crab Quiches
  Chocolate Fondue with fruits
 *Cheesecake Squares

60-100 people — late afternoon or evening

  Ham with biscuits
  Fresh turkey with small rolls
  Roast beef with small rolls
 *Lumpia with sauces
**Mornay Sauce with crabclaws and shrimp
  Crab-Clam Spread with crackers (double batch)
**Colorful Mexican Dip with tortilla chips
**Frito Beef-Bean Dip with tortilla chips
**Fresh Vegetables with Dill Dip and Curry Dip
**Fresh Garlic Herb Cheese with crackers
 *Zucchini Squares (3 batches)
 *Petite Pecan Tarts
 *Brownie Mounds

*FREEZABLE

**CAN BE PREPARED AT LEAST TWO DAYS AHEAD

Quiet "Sit-By-The-Fire Dinner" for 4-6:

Dinner #1:

> Artichoke Heart Cheese Dip with Tortilla Chips
> Polynesian Chicken Wings
> Mexican Pinwheels
> Peanut-Butter Chocolate Bars

Dinner #2:

> Potato Skins with Dip
> Hawaiian Sausage Balls
> Parmesan-Garlic Shrimp
> Strawberry Fondue

Dinner #3:

> Swiss Cheese Dip with Vegetables
> Hot Bean Dip with tortilla chips
> Celery Victor
> Stuffed Mushrooms
> Caramel Brownies

Dinner #4:

> Cheese Toast Canapes
> Tuna Onion Dip with vegetables and crackers
> Nachos with Guacamole
> Bacon-Mushroom Wraps
> Brownie Mounds

Dinner #5:

> Sausalito Sourdoughs
> Supreme Sausages
> Dill Dip with vegetables
> Chocolate Fondue with fresh fruits

For the Teen Scene —
Favorites For The Fussy

Hormel Chili Cheese Dip with Tortilla Chips
Chili Con Quesa with Tortilla Chips
Swiss Cheese Dip with Vegetables
Holiday Cheese Ball with crackers
Party Mix
Clam Dip with Potato Chips
Sour Dough Shrimp Dip
Cheese Toast Canapes
Polynesian Chicken Wings
Potato Skins with Dip
Mexican Pinwheels
Nachos and Tostada Dip
Mexican Meatballs

Chocolate fondue is high on the sweets list, however, all the "sweet part of the party" recipes will be a hit.

Index

Almond Roca, 81

Amaretto Fondue, 78

Apricot Squares, 85

Armenian Canapes, 35

ARTICHOKES
Artichoke Cheese Dip, 10
Artichokes in Blue Cheese, 52
Artichoke Squares, 40
Crab-Artichoke-Mushroom
Appetizer, 65

Asparagus Rolls, 49

AVOCADOS
Avocado Crab Dip, 66
Avocado Crab Quiche, 47
Guacamole I, 11
Guacamole, II, 11
Nachos, 38
Tostada Dip, 15

BACON
Bacon Cheese Toast Canapes, 49
Bacon Mushroom Wraps, 60
Bacon Wraps, 52
Quiche Lorraine, 45

BEANS
Frito Beef Bean Dip, 14
Hot Bean Dip, 12
Tostada Dip, 15

BEEF
Beef Cheese Ball, 28
Chipped Beef Spreads, 25
Korean Beef with Vegetables, 57
Mexican Meatballs, 53
Sausage Treats, 22

Blue Pecan Mushrooms, 59

Braunschweiger Spread Dip, 23

Bricks of Cream Cheese, 76

Broccoli-Mushroom-Cheese Dip, 13

Broiled Chicken on Rye, 41

Brownie Mounds, 84

Caramel Brownies, 79

Celery Victor, 56

Cheesecake Squares, 80

CHEESES
Beef Cheese Ball, 28
Bricks of Cream Cheese, 76
Broccoli Mushroom Cheese
Dip, 13
Cheesecake Squares, 80
Cheese 'N Chutney Ball, 29
Cheese Nut Mushrooms, 58
Cheese Rolls, 34
Cheese Toast Canapes, 43
Garlic Herb Cheese, 28
Hot Cheese Crab, 68
Chili Cheese Dip, 11
Chili Cheese Squares, 44
Chili Con Queso, 12
Mango Chutney Cheese Pate, 24
Smoke Salmon on Boursin, 42
Swiss Cheese Dip, 18

CHICKEN
Broiled Chicken on Rye, 41
Polynesian Chicken Wings, 37
Spinach Chicken with Oriental
Dip, 54

CHILI
Chili Cheese Dip, 11
Chili Con Queso, 12

Chipped Beef Spreads, 25

CHOCOLATE
Almond Roca, 81
Brownie Mounds, 84
Caramel Brownies, 79
Chocolate Cups, 83
Chocolate Fondue, 78
Peanut Butter Chocolate Bars, 81
Peppermint Brownies, 82

CLAMS
Crab-Clam Spread, 69
Clam Dip for Potato Chips, 68

Colorful Mexican Dip, 14

CRAB
Avocado Crab Dip, 66
Crab and Water Chestnut
Spread, 63
Crab-Artichoke-Mushroom
Appetizer, 65
Crab-Clam Spread, 69
Crabmeat Canapes, 36

Crabmeat Cocktail Block, 64
Crab or Shrimp Mold, 66
Crab Rolls, 34
Fruits de Mer, 70
Hot Cheese Crab Dip, 68
King Crab Spread, 69
Mornay Sauce for Crab Claws
    and Shrimp, 62
Sausalito Sourdoughs, 41
Cream Cheese Pastry, 88
Cucumber Dip, 20

CURRY
Curried Mushroom Rolls, 33
Curry Dip, 19

Dates, sherried, 74
Dill Weed Dip, 20

Easy Escargots, 75

FONDUES
Amaretto Fondue, 78
Chocolate Fondue, 78
Pineapple Fluff, 83
Strawberry Fundue, 86
Swiss Cheese Dip for
    Vegetables, 18
Fresh Garlic Herb Cheese, 28
Frito Beef Bean Chili Dip, 14
Fruitboat, 78
Fruits de Mer, 70

Garlic Herb Cheese, 28
Green Chili Salsa, 89
Guacamole, 11

Ham Pinwheels, 74
Hawaiian Sausage Balls, 55
Holiday Cheese Ball, 29
Hot Bean Dip, 12
Hot Cheese Crab, 68

King Crab Spread, 69
Korean Beef with Vegetables, 57

LIVER
Braunschweiger, 23
Rumaki Spread, 22
Lumpia with Shrimp and Pork, 39

Mango Chutney Cheese Pate, 24
Marinated Mushrooms, 60

MEATBALLS
Hawaiian Sausage Balls, 55
Mexican Meatballs, 53
Mexican Dip, 14
Mexican Meatballs, 53
Mexican Pinwheels, 43
Mornay Sauce for Crab Claws and
    Shrimp, 62

MUSHROOMS
Bacon Cheese Mushrooms, 58
Blue Pecan Mushrooms, 59
Broccoli-Mushroom Cheese
    Dip, 13
Cheese Nut Mushrooms, 58
Crab-Artichoke-Mushroom
    Appetizer, 65
Marinated Mushrooms, 60
Oriental Mushrooms, 59
Mustard Dip, 19

Nachos, 38

Olive Wraps, 52
Oysters Bluepoint, 70

Parmesan Garlic Shrimp, 71
Party Mix, 75
Pastry, cream cheese pastry
    crust, 88
Peanut Butter Chocolate Bars, 81
Pecan: petite pecan tarts, 79
Peppermint Brownies, 82
Petite Pecan Tarts, 79
Phyllo Dough, 32
Pineapple Fluff Dip, 83
Pink Shrimp Mousse, 67
Polynesian Chicken Wings, 37

PORK
Hawaiian Sausage Balls, 55
Lumpia with Shrimp and
    Pork, 39
Potato Skins, 36

QUICHES
Avocado Crab Quiche, 47
Quiche Lorraine, 45
Zucchini Quiche, 46

Rumaki Spread, 22

Salami Onion Rolls, 74

SALMON
Salmon Party Log, 67
Smoked Salmon and Boursin on
Cucumbers, 42

SAUSAGE
Hawaiian Sausage Balls, 55
Supreme Sausages, 56
Sausage Treats, 22

Sausalito Sourdoughs, 41

SCALLOPS
Seviche, 72

Seviche, 72

Sherried Dates, 74

SHRIMP
Fruits de Mer, 70
Lumpia with Shrimp and
Pork, 39
Mornay Sauce for Shrimp and
Crab, 62
Pink Shrimp Mousse, 67
Shrimp filling for Cherry
Tomatoes, 48
Shrimp or Crab Mold, 66
Sourdough Shrimp Dip, 63

Smoke Salmon and Boursin on
Cucumbers, 42

Sourdough Shrimp Dip, 63

SPINACH
Spinach Chicken with Oriental
Dip, 54
Spinach Dip, 23
Spinach Rolls, 35
Spinach Squares, 37

Strawberry Fundue, 86

**STUFFERS FOR
CHERRY TOMATOES**
Curried Tuna, 48
Shrimp Filling, 48

Supreme Sausages, 56

Sweet and Sour Sauce, 88

Swiss Cheese Dip, 18

TOMATOES, CHERRY
Curried tuna filling, 48
Shrimp filling, 48
Dip: A Colorful Mexican Dip, 14
Sauce: Green Chili Salsa, 89

Tortilla Chips, 10

Tostada Dip, 15

TUNA
Curried Tuna, 48
Tuna Onion Spread, 18

ZUCCHINI
Zucchini Bars, 40
Zucchini Quiche, 46
Zucchini Rounds, 42
Susan's Zucchini Snacks, 76